LANCASTER COUNTY PENNSYLVANIA BUCKET LIST

1OO WAYS TO HAVE A REAL LANCASTER COUNTY EXPERIENCE

ANGELA R RUHL

ISBN– 13:

978–1539968825

ISBN– 10:

1539968820

The use of a city, state or geographic region in conjunction with Bucket List is a trademark ™ for books in a series. If you would like to write or publish a Bucket List for your locale please contact the author of The Ocean City New Jersey Bucket List: Maryann.Bolen@gmail.com. She will be happy to help you get started.

legal disclaimer

This book is designed to provide information, entertainment, and motivation to our readers. It is sold with the understanding that the publisher is not engaged to render any type of physical, psychological, legal or any other kind of professional advice.

Participation in the activities listed may be dangerous or illegal and could lead to arrest, serious injury, or death.

The content of this book is the sole expression and opinion of its author and not necessarily that of the publisher. No warranties or guarantees are expressed or implied.

Neither the publisher nor the individual author shall be liable for any physical, psychological, emotional, financial, or commercial damages, including, but not limited to, special, incidental, consequential, or other damages.

Our views and rights are the same: you are responsible for your own choices, actions, and results.

dedication

To my rock, my motivation, my inspiration, my
strength..... my daughter. Thank you for your love
and support. Don't just believe your dreams can
come true but make them come true. Take the
high road with your head held high. Push forward
with confidence.

To my family.... especially my mom & step-dad,
Grandma Lyanna, my sister Jamie & Trey , my
brother Dan, Marissa & the boys and Jordan.
Thank you for your unconditional love and support.
This book was written because you believed in me.

To my friends who surrounded me and supported
me through my highs and lows. I would not be
where I am today without you. Thank you for the
gift of your friendship.

To those who have helped and are helping me
check things off the Ocean City NJ Bucket List
books. Cherished memories have been made and I
look forward to many more.

acknowledgements

Thank you to Bob & Mary Ann Bolen for writing the Ocean City, New Jersey Bucket List books which inspired me to write my own. Thank you for all your support and guidance.

Thank you to my "Tech" people, Charles & Melissa Melhorn for always being there and helping me when I was in a panic.

Thank you to everyone who helped me with ideas and made this book possible.

Cover photo credit to Brianna Myers.

Cover designs and county maps credit to Jamie Ober.

Family photo credit to Laurie Ober

Family photo edit credit to Trey Horsey

why a bucket list?

One spring evening on our annual family weekend in Ocean City, New Jersey I was looking through the Bucket List books that were written about Ocean City. While reminiscing about all the memories these books created with my family and friends I found myself thinking about writing my own book to help others create memories in my home county.

In our Bucket List books we write the date, who participated in the activity and my grandma attempts to draw something that pertains to the activity we achieved. Sometimes this in itself brings lots of laughter! I often look through the books and feel blessed and inspired by all the things we have achieved together.

My goal is for you to create lifetime memories like we have with family and friends. Enjoy your time in Lancaster County! Blessings on your adventures!

Angela.Ruhl@hotmail.com

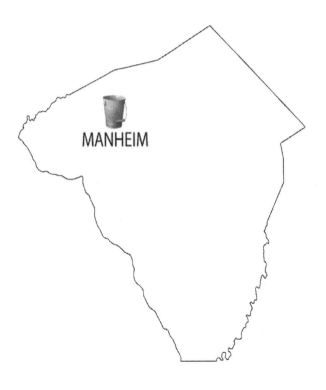

MANHEIM

Cat's Meow

Learn the history of this
restaurant while
enjoying your favorite
flavor of wings

Did you know???

This restaurant was formally named
American House Railroad Hotel

Manheim Railway Station

Learn of the heritage of Manheim, trolleys and trains in Lancaster County

Did you know???

This station was constructed in 1881

Twin Kiss

Enjoy a Hot Roast Beef
dinner and a frosted mug of
homemade root beer.
During the winter months,
try some homemade
Chicken Pot Pie! Don't
forget to end your meal
with some delicious
ice cream!

Pennsylvania Renaissance Faire

Stroll back in time and
enjoy one of the many
themed weekends

Did you know???

The Ren Faire covers 35 acres.

Pinch Pond Campground

Spend quality time with family and friends while enjoying the activities at this home away from home

Did you know???

Pinch Pond has been family owned and operated for over 40 years

Mount Hope
Estate & Winery

Take a tour through
this 19th century mansion
and the wine shop. Don't
forget to take a break in the
wine tasting room!

Did you know???

The wine that is sold here is made from
Pennsylvania grown fruit

Kreider Farms

Take a Tour of Kreider Farms and climb the Silo Observation Tower

Did you know???

Established in 1935, Kreider Farms currently has 1900 cows in their herd; 1700 of which are milked three times a day. They have 1900 young stock, which are currently not milked. They also have 6.5 million laying chickens some of which are cage free and cage free organic

Take time out of your
busy schedule to drive
around with the family to
find Christmas lights!!

Town Clock

The clock was brought to town by jeweler Harry Flinchbaugh in 1926 from a jewelry store in Lancaster. It is now owned by the Manheim Historical Society and moved to this location in 1994.

Did you know???

The clock keeps current time by winding it once a week!

The Keath House

Learn the history of
one of the oldest
houses in Manheim

Did you know???

This house was named after Peter Keath, a
blacksmith who purchased the property in
1887

Roots Farmers Market

Enjoy some local fruits,
vegetables and a
cheesesteak from
Steaks N Stuff

Did you know???

Roots was founded in 1925 by A.W Root

Fasig House

Visit the house where
early church
congregations held their
first meetings

Did you know???

In 1974, this log house was relocated from
South Charlotte Street to East High Street

Stiegel Glassworks
1976

Experience how pieces of glass are manufactured using the traditional techniques of 1762

Did you know???

Valuable pieces are on display at Manheim
Railroad Station Museum, Corning Glass
and the Hershey Museum

Before leaving

Manheim...

You must

_____

LITITZ

High Sports

Spend the afternoon
playing miniature golf,
go-kart driving, hitting at
the batting cages or at the
driving range

Wilbur Chocolate

Enjoy some Wilbur Buds
as you learn the history of
their origin

Did you know???

The Wilbur Bud was created in 1894 by
Henry Oscar Wilbur

Welcome Center/Train Station

Gather all the information you need to enjoy your time in this beautiful town

Did you know???

Lititz was voted "America's Coolest Small Town" in 2013

Penn Cinema

Enjoy the latest movies
and IMAX while
grabbing a snack and
getting off your feet

Did you know???

Penn Cinema opened its Lititz location in
2006 and opened a second location in
Wilmington, Delaware in 2012

Downtown

Enjoy the day with a walk through the town and check out all the unique shops along the way!

Did you know???

There are over 70 independently owned shops and restaurants in downtown Lititz

Julius Sturgis Pretzel Factory

Tour the original bakery and twist your own pretzel

Did you know???

Sturgis Pretzel was founded in 1861

Lititz Springs Park

Enjoy the 4th of July
festivities and fireworks
from the park

Did you know???

The park is a privately owned park. It is
owned by the Lititz Moravian
Congregation and maintained by the
Churches of Lititz.

Moravian Church
& Museum

Discover the display of paintings,
musical instruments and artifacts
from the congregation that
established this town as a church
community in 1756

Did you know???

The Moravian Brothers house that was
built in 1759 was approved to serve as a
hospital during the American
Revolutionary War

Lancaster Airport

Watch the planes and
helicopters take off and
land while grabbing a
bite to eat at Fiorentino's

Did you know???

This airport started out as a private airport.
180 acres of farmland was purchased to
convert it to a municipal airport

Wolf Sanctuary

This sanctuary of over 80 plus acres provides shelter, food and veterinary care without any government or corporate assistance. Your donation matters!

Did you know???

You can "adopt a wolf" from the sanctuary

Lititz Family Cupboard

Enjoy a delicious variety of food from the menu or the buffet

Did you know???

You could receive a free meal for your birthday! (Don't forget you ID)

Bulls Head Public House

Relax with a drink from the pub that is modeled after a traditional British pub

Did you know???

Bulls Head has been recognized as the
"best beer bar in Pennsylvania"

Oregon Dairy

Purchase a deliciously
fresh made cake from the
award-winning bakery

Did you know???

The original farm was purchased in 1952

Family Farm
Days
at Oregon Dairy

Take a tractor or hay ride,
visit the dairy barn or
scramble though hay
tunnels!

Did you know???

This family event is free

Before leaving
Lititz…

You must

_____

LANCASTER

Lancaster Barnstormers

Participate in singing "Take Me Out To The Ballgame" during the 7th inning stretch

Did you know???

The Barnstormers stadium is called Clipper Magazine Stadium and opened in 2003

Penn Square

Visit the statue in the middle of the square known as the Soldiers and Sailors Monument

Did you know???

Lancaster was capital of the United States for one day in 1777

Support a nonprofit animal organization in Lancaster County

Did you know???

Giving an animal a forever home is a great way to support homeless animals but you can also volunteer your time or make a donation

The Outlets

Find a great deal at
Tanger and Rockvale

Dutch Wonderland

Enjoy this 48 acre amusement park known as the "Kingdom for Kids"

Did you know???

This park was opened in 1963 by a potato farmer named Earl Clark. Hershey Entertainment and Resort company purchased the park in 2001

Rock Ford Plantation

Tour the home of Revolutionary War General Edward Hand

Did you know???

The mansion is on the National Register of Historic Places

Tours of Wheatland

Tour the home of our 15th President
- James Buchanan -

Did you know???

James Buchanan was the only President
from Pennsylvania and the only President
to remain a lifelong bachelor

American Music Theatre

Escape the hustle and bustle and relax at a concert or show

Did you know???

AMT hosts 300 live performances a year

Central Market

Shop for farm-fresh produce, fruit, dairy or meat on a Tuesday, Friday or Saturday

Did you know???

Until 2005, this market was the oldest municipally operated market in the United States

Long's Park

Participate in one of the many activities this park has to offer. Summer Concert Series, Art and Craft Festival, World's Largest Chicken Barbecue, etc

Did you know???

The park also has picnic pavilions, a petting farm, children's playgrounds, a spring fed lake, tennis courts and a fitness trail

Ask a local how to properly pronounce Lancaster

Did you know???

Lancaster's nickname is the Red Rose City

Learn how to play Dutch Blitz in one of Lancaster County Parks on a beautiful day

Did you know???

Dutch Blitz was created by Werner Ernst George Muller, a German immigrant from Bucks County, Pennsylvania

Lancaster Brewing Company

Take a tour to see brewing operations

Did you know???

The building that now houses Lancaster Brewing Company was once the historic Edward McGovern Tobacco Warehouse

Lancaster Science Factory

Enjoy hands-on interactive technology and science center while exploring exhibits relating to engineering, physical sciences, mathematics and technology

Did you know???

James Bunting founded the Science Factory with the goal to increase children's interests in math and science

North Museum of Nature and Science

Participate in a SciDome Theater show

Did you know???

The museum was founded in 1953 by
Franklin & Marshall College

Chameleon Club

Get your game on in The Lizard Lounge while waiting for your concert to start

Did you know???

3 Doors Down, Green Eggs, August Burns Red, Buckcherry, Gavin DeGraw, Live and Shinedown are just a few who have performed here

Go 'N Bananas

Plenty of fun at this family fun center. Arcade games, mini bowling, laser tag and more

Fulton Theatre

Enjoy a musical, play or concert

Did you know???

This building was named after Robert Fulton, a Lancaster County steam engine pioneer

Lost Treasure
Golf and Maze

Play a competitive round of mini-golf. The loser buys ice cream!

Did you know???

The Lost Treasure also has courses in 5 other states

Boettcher House Museum

Stroll through this 70-acre natural habitat with trails.

Did you know???

This house was built in 1920

Lancaster's First Friday

Join the crowds...check out the galleries and listen to the street musicians

Susquehannock
State Park

Look for hawks, eagles
and migratory birds
while taking a hike

Take a piece of Lancaster County home with you from a "Mud" Sale

Did you know???

Non-Amish are called "English"

Discover where
Lancaster's nickname,
"The Red Rose City"
originated from

Before leaving

Lancaster...

You must

_____

COLUMBIA

Turkey Hill Experience

Create your own virtual ice cream flavor, sample ice cream & iced tea and learn how ice cream is made

Did you know???

The grand opening of The Turkey Hill Experience took place on June 4, 2011

National Clock and Watch Museum

View over 12,000 collection items

Did you know???

The museum opened in 1977 with fewer than 1,000 items

First National Bank Museum

Tour this museum that has the original 1800's setting

Did you know???

The First National Bank of Columbia was chartered in 1864

Wright's Ferry Mansion

Tour the restored home built in 1738 for Quaker Susanna Wright

Did you know???

Susanna helped establish colonial self-sufficiency

Breezy View Outlook

Enjoy a picnic while taking in the breathtaking view of the Susquehanna River, Columbia & Chiques Rock

Did you know???

The Susquehanna River is 464 miles long and is the longest river on the American east coast that drains into the Atlantic Ocean

Before leaving
Columbia…

You must

_____

LANDISVILLE

Herr Family Homestead

1852 brick farmhouse and A style post-and beam barn exhibits items from the 80 year life of Amos Herr

Did you know???

The Amos Herr house and family homestead is an excellent example of a Lancaster County non-Amish farm in the mid-19th century

Miss Calee's Eats -N- Treats

Enjoy a home style meal and some homemade peanut butter fudge

Did you know???

The restaurant is named after a family member

Before leaving
Landisville...

You must

_____

BIRD-IN-HAND

Bird-in-Hand Family Restaurant

Satisfy your sweet tooth with a Whoopie Pie

Did you know???

Most of the food is made from scratch with in season produce coming from local Amish & Mennonite farms as well as the beef & poultry coming from local producers

The Amish Experience at Plain & Fancy Farm

Learn about the Amish of now and then

Did you know???

This is the home of the only "experiential" theater on the east coast

Before leaving
Bird in Hand...

You must

_____

EPHRATA

Ephrata Cloister

Tour the 18th-century Brothers and Sisters houses that are not only a historic landmark but are also monuments to religious freedom

Did you know???

The Cloister was a tight-knit community of believers who lived an ascetic and celibate life

Ephrata Fair

Indulge in some good
food and fun games at
this week long event

Did you know???

Wednesday is parade night

Udder Choice

Enjoy some good food at this family owned restaurant. Don't forget your ice cream for dessert

Did you know???

The Udder Choice has homemade ice cream

Weaver Nut Company

Pick up a snack for the road. Choose from candy, dried fruit, nuts, sweets, bulk foods and more

Did you know???

This is a family owned and operated business since 1975

Isaac's Restaurant & Deli

Choose a menu item named after a bird or a flower

Did you know???

Isaac's is a local chain restaurant that opened in 1983

Before leaving
Ephrata…

You must

_____

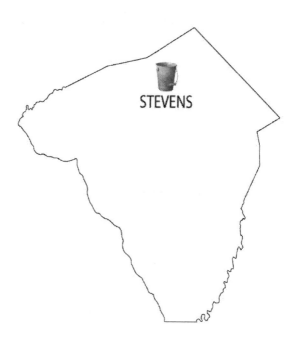

STEVENS

Refreshing Mountain Zipline

Challenge yourself by zipping from platform to platform. If feeling brave, take on the course with challenging elements

Did you know???

Refreshing Mountain also offers a Climbing Tower, Slingshots, Pedal Carts, Paintball Targets, camping and more

The Penguin Hotel

Satisfy your thirst and hunger at this kid friendly country bar/restaurant

Did you know???

The history behind The Penguin Hotel dates back to 1763

Before leaving

Stevens...

You must

_____

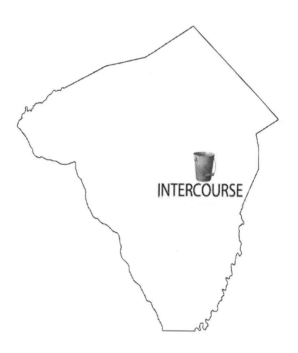

INTERCOURSE

Kitchen Kettle Village

Spend the day browsing through the more than 40 merchants this village has to offer

Did you know???

The owners started out over 60 years ago with a jelly business

Be adventurous and take
a drive on back country
roads to admire the
beauty of the countryside
and farmland

Before leaving

Intercourse...

You must

_____

EAST EARL

Shady Maple Smorgasbord

Satisfy everyone's hunger
with over 100 daily items
to choose from

Did you know???

You can get a free buffet for your birthday!
(Don't forget your ID)

Horst's
Greenhouse

Take home a piece of
Lancaster County by taking
home a plant or flowers

Did you know???

Horst's is a family owned business that
opened their doors in April of 1994

Before leaving

East Earl…

You must

_____

STRASBURG

National Toy Train Museum

Enjoy the world-class collection of toy trains for kids of all ages

Did you know???

It has been said that this museum is believed to be the largest publicly exhibited toy and model train collection in the United States

Village Greens Miniature Golf & Snack Shoppe

Show your skill at one or both of these beautiful courses that covers over 13 acres

Did you know???

Village Greens has been voted #1
miniature golf course in Lancaster County
by readers of Lancaster County Magazine
for 5 consecutive years

Sight & Sound Theatre

Enjoy the breathe taking
show of the season.
Prepare to be amazed at
the live performance.

Did you know???

This is the largest faith-based live theatre
in the country and has been described as
"Christian Broadway."

Before leaving

Strasburg...

You must

_____

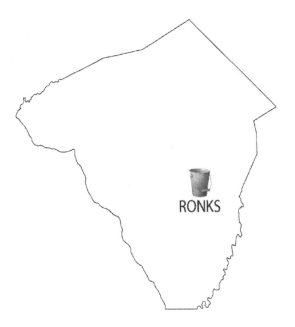

RONKS

Cherry Crest Adventure Farm

Ready to test your sense of direction? Work your way through the Amazing Maize Maze

Did you know???

This property dated back to the 1700's as a working farm and was owned by a family who came from France to escape religious persecution.

The Lil' Country Store & Miniature Horse Farm

Pet a miniature pony and take a selfie with one

Did you know???

The products are Amish crafted and made on the farm

Strasburg Railroad

Take a 9 mile roundtrip excursion on a restored train car pulled by a historic steam engine

Did you know???

You can ride with classic storybook friend Thomas the Tank Engine

Before leaving

Ronks...

You must

_____

WILLOW STREET

Hans Herr House & Lancaster Longhouse

Take in the sun while touring this outdoor complex with an agriculture museum

Did you know???

This is the oldest Mennonite Church in North America and Lancaster County's oldest building

Boehm's Chapel

Visit the site that was purchased by Swiss Mennonites in 1710 from William Penn

Did you know???

This Chapel was the first Methodist Church in Lancaster County and it is the oldest existing structure built for Methodist worship in Pennsylvania and the fourth in the nation

Before leaving

Willow Street...

You must

_____

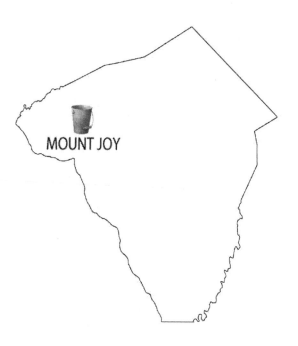

MOUNT JOY

Bube's Brewery

Take a tour of the catacombs

Did you know???

Bube's offers Live Music, Trivia Night,
Murder Mystery Dinners and more

Vineyard at Grandview

Enjoy wine tasting at this award winning winery

Did you know???

Vineyard at Grandview won 5 awards at the San Francisco International Wine Competition in 2016

Cyclones

Hang out and support this awesome football team

Did you know???

The Cyclones had a 10–0 record in their 2016 season

Before leaving

Mount Joy...

You must

_____

MARIETTA

River Trail

Enjoy the wildlife and farmland while walking/jogging or bicycling this 14 mile trail that spans through 5 municipalities

Did you know???

Marietta was formerly know as Anderson's Ferry

McCleary's Irish Pub

Enjoy a glass of wine or a beer during Happy Hour

Did you know???

McCleary's can also host and cater your parties, banquets, and family gatherings

Marietta Day

Attend this fun filled day in May by supporting local vendors, playing games, eating some great food and enjoying the music

Did you know???

Marietta was founded in 1718 by Scots-Irish immigrants and was formed by the alliance of four separate settlements

Before leaving

Marietta...

You must

_____

I did it.....

–Manheim

- ☐ Cat's Meow
- ☐ Manheim Railway/Station
- ☐ Twin Kiss
- ☐ Pennsylvania Renaissance Faire
- ☐ Pinch Pond Campground
- ☐ Mount Hope Estate
- ☐ Kreider Farms
- ☐ Christmas lights
- ☐ Town Clock
- ☐ Keath House
- ☐ Roots Farmers Market
- ☐ Fasig House
- ☐ Stiegel Glassworks 1976
- ☐ Before leaving Manheim...

–Lititz

- ☐ High Sports
- ☐ Wilber Chocolate
- ☐ Welcome Center/Train Station
- ☐ Penn Cinema
- ☐ Downtown
- ☐ Julius Sturgis Pretzel Factory
- ☐ Lititz Springs Park
- ☐ Moravian Church & Museum
- ☐ Lancaster Airport
- ☐ Wolf Sanctuary
- ☐ Lititz Family Cupboard
- ☐ Bullshead Public House
- ☐ Oregon Dairy
- ☐ Family Farm Days at Oregon Dairy
- ☐ Before leaving Lititz...

–Lancaster

- ☐ Lancaster Barnstormers
- ☐ Penn Square
- ☐ Support a non profit animal organization
- ☐ Outlets
- ☐ Dutch Wonderland
- ☐ Rockford Plantation
- ☐ Tours of Wheatland
- ☐ American Music Theatre
- ☐ Central Market
- ☐ Long's Park
- ☐ Pronounce Lancaster
- ☐ Dutch Blitz
- ☐ Lancaster Brewing Company
- ☐ Lancaster Science Factory
- ☐ North Museum
- ☐ Chameleon Club
- ☐ Go 'N Bananas
- ☐ Fulton Theatre

- ☐ Lost Treasure Golf & Maze
- ☐ Boettcher House Museum
- ☐ Lancaster First Friday
- ☐ Susquehannok State Park
- ☐ Mud Sale
- ☐ Lancaster's Nickname
- ☐ Before leaving Lancaster...

-Columbia

- ☐ Turkey Hill Experience
- ☐ National Clock & Watch Museum
- ☐ First National Bank Museum
- ☐ Wright's Ferry Mansion
- ☐ Breezy View Outlook
- ☐ Before leaving Columbia...

- Landisville

- ☐ Herr Family Homestead
- ☐ Miss Calee's Eats N Treats
- ☐ Before leaving Landisville...

–Bird In Hand

- ☐ Bird In Hand Family Restaurant
- ☐ Plain & Fancy Farm
- ☐ Before leaving Bird In Hand...

–Ephrata

- ☐ Ephrata Cloister
- ☐ Ephrata Fair
- ☐ Udder Choice
- ☐ Weaver Nut Company
- ☐ Isaac's Restaurant & Deli
- ☐ Before leaving Ephrata...

–Stevens

- ☐ Refreshing Mountain Zipline
- ☐ The Penguin Hotel
- ☐ Before leaving Stevens...

–Intercourse

- ☐ Kitchen Kettle Village
- ☐ Drive on back country roads
- ☐ Before leaving Intercourse...

-East Earl

- ☐ Shady Maple Smorgasboard
- ☐ Horst's Greenhouse
- ☐ Before leaving East Earl...

-Strasburg

- ☐ National Toy Train Museum
- ☐ Village Green Mini Golf
- ☐ Sight & Sound
- ☐ Before leaving Strasburg...

-Ronks

- ☐ Cherry Crest
- ☐ Lil' Country Store
- ☐ Strasburg Railroad
- ☐ Before leaving Ronks...

-Willow Street

- ☐ Hans Herr House
- ☐ Boehm's Chapel
- ☐ Before leaving Willow Street...

-Mount Joy

- ☐ Bube's Brewery
- ☐ Vineyard at Grandview
- ☐ Cyclones
- ☐ Before leaving Mount Joy...

-Marietta

- ☐ River Trail
- ☐ McCleary's Irish Pub
- ☐ Marietta Day
- ☐ Before leaving Marietta...

Books in the
Bucket List Series:

If you would like to write a "Bucket List" about your area, contact Mary Ann at MaryAnnBolen@gmail.com and she would be happy to help you get started.

Made in the USA
San Bernardino, CA
18 February 2017